CW01513328

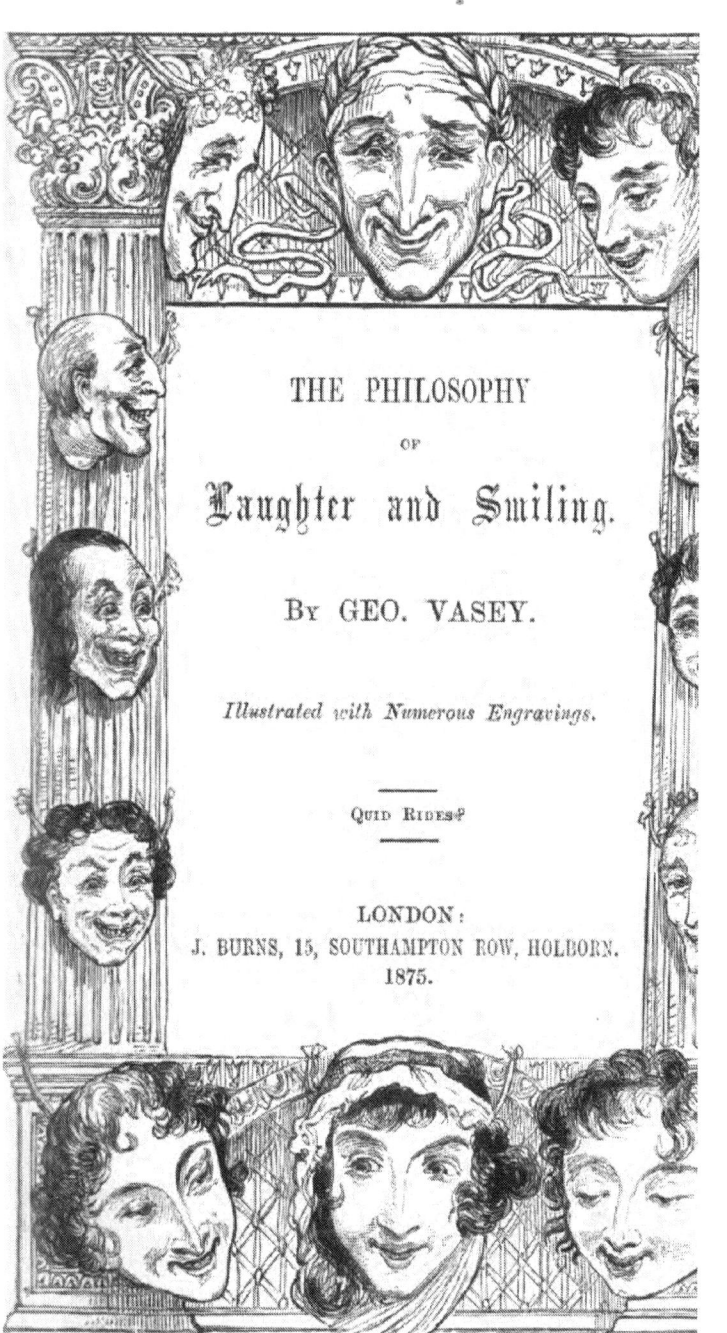

THE PHILOSOPHY

OF

Laughter and Smiling.

By GEO. VASEY.

Illustrated with Numerous Engravings.

QUID RIDES?

LONDON:
J. BURNS, 15, SOUTHAMPTON ROW, HOLBORN.
1875.

TO THE

INTELLIGENT, THOUGHTFUL, AND REFLECTING,

OF EVERY RANK AND STATION,

THIS LITTLE BOOK

IS RESPECTFULLY DEDICATED.

PREFACE.

ALTHOUGH its subject is laughter, the present volume is by no means a *jest-book*. Quite the contrary. In the following pages this subject is investigated carefully and elaborately, and with all the seriousness and gravity becoming a scientific or philosophical inquiry.

The phenomenon of laughter is brought into the field of vision in all its most important phases—anatomical, physiological, intellectual, and moral, by which it will be perceived that the subject of laughter is " no laughing matter."

It must, however, be confessed that, not-withstanding a considerable amount both of time and labour has been expended in the composition of the following essay, it is yet only a rough outline of this very important and interesting subject, which may, by further elaboration—(if time and oppor-tunity permit)—be wrought out into a much more complete treatise.

I shall, nevertheless, have accomplished my present object if I merely succeed in drawing public attention to the facts which I have brought forward, and to the great probability of the inferences which I have ventured to suggest, so as to induce the intelligent and observing to give them a due amount of consideration.

Next in importance to those who have been the means of establishing truths worthy of acceptance, may be ranked those

who discover and point out opinions worthy
of examination.

In making these few prefatory remarks
. I feel forcibly prompted to deprecate that
particular amount of adverse criticism
which, under ordinary circumstances, might
fairly be applied to several parts of the following sketch. I allude to the many repe-
titions which I have thought it necessary
to make in illustration of my theory.

I have no doubt that this tautology will
be condemned in the most emphatic manner
by many of my readers who are blessed with
retentive memories, and who read carefully ;
but the great majority of readers do not
possess these important qualifications.

Moreover, I may be allowed to state that
my theme is so entirely novel—I may say
unique — and the opinions which I have
ventured to advance are so diametrically

opposed to those which are universally entertained on the subject, that I felt compelled, in justice to my argument, to make use of considerable reiteration.

If I need further exculpation, I can safely shelter myself under the authority and example of no less a dignitary than the famous Archbishop Fénélon.

On one occasion this great man was at a large party, in which were several superficial critics, who gave utterance to some rather depreciating remarks on the Archbishop having repeated himself in certain of his literary productions.

He modestly requested to have the passages pointed out to which allusion had been made. This was very readily done. " Ah," said he, " I perceive you recollect the passages ; and *that they might be recollected was my reason for repeating them.*"

TABLE OF CONTENTS.

———◦◦◦———

I respectfully request the reader to bear this in mind.

The principal illustrations have been executed by the Brothers Taylor, so well known as first-rate portrait-engravers. Their excellence requires no eulogium.

G. VASEY.

May, 1875.

PAGE.

CHAPTER VII.

CHAPTER VIII.

CHAPTER IX.

CHAPTER X.

CHAPTER XI.

b

PAGE.

CHAPTER XX.

CHAPTER XXI.

CHAPTER XXII.

CHAPTER XXIII.

CHAPTER XXIV.

APPENDIX,

COLLATERAL AND EXPLANATORY.

———•◦•———

INTRODUCTION.

———◦•◦———

It will be freely granted by all those who observe and reflect that every community of human beings (more especially those which consider themselves civilised) practise a thousand habits, and entertain ten thousand opinions, of which they can give no rational account.

This, however, will cease to excite our astonishment when we consider that all the knowledge we receive, as well as all the habits we contract, are received and contracted with the most unreserved confidence, without doubting, questioning, or even reflecting.

B

Be it observed, moreover, that the mechanical parrot-and-monkey training which is now so universal is commenced and incessantly persevered in, long before we are at all capable of discriminating between that which is good and that which is evil—between that which is true and that which is false—and, consequently, before we are able to judge or determine whether the knowledge which we are receiving, and the habits we are acquiring, are true and beneficial or false and injurious.

Under these unfavourable circumstances we would suggest that one of the happiest, as well as one of the most important, ideas which can enter the minds of those who are earnestly endeavouring to acquire true knowledge (after having been instructed in the ordinary routine methods) is that of reviewing all their previously-acquired knowledge, of doubting and questioning whether or not they have been properly taught, and of determining boldly, but carefully, to investigate the truth for themselves.

In this self-investigation we undoubtedly labour under a very great disadvantage—namely, that of being imbued and surrounded by a host of prejudices—in other words, of judgments formed without examination—and these it behoves us absolutely to renounce if we sincerely desire to obtain clear, distinct, and correct knowledge.

To enable us to overcome this difficulty in the most effectual manner (after having acquired some amount of experience and judgment), we must, in the first place, carefully take stock of all our kinds and degrees of knowledge, and give them a thorough revision.

In the second place, we must entirely banish those principles and habits which we discover to be false, superstitious, or prejudicial, and retain only such as we find on examination to be true in principle and beneficial in practice.

Moreover, we must bear in mind that our social and domestic habits are invariably the result of public opinion, and we must never forget that public opinion is chiefly founded on ignorance or very imperfect knowledge, the result of which is that our daily habits are frequently of the most injurious character; bear witness the misery, the vice, the folly, the crime which unfortunately ramify through all classes of society, the great mass of which evils is the consequence of a grossly ignorant public opinion.

The present essay is a humble but earnest attempt to investigate the nature and question the propriety of opinions which are all but 'universal upon the subject of a habit which is extremely prevalent, and which, in Christendom at least, is regarded with unanimous complacence and approbation.

It must not be supposed for a moment that the Author has the most distant idea of effecting, by means of the following essay, any intellectual or moral revolution; but he feels tolerably confident that his suggestions will excite in the minds of the thoughtful a persistent train of rational reflection.

THE PHILOSOPHY

OF

LAUGHTER AND SMILING.

———

CHAPTER I.

First—On the pecuniary expense of laughter. *Second*
—On those who are enriched by it. *Third*—On
its imagined advantages and benefits.

1. IT is assuredly a great fact, which cannot be gainsayed, that an immense majority
of the inhabitants of most civilised countries
hold the habit of laughing in such high esti-
mation, and feel such a craving for the exercise of it, that collectively they expend vast
sums of money in procuring the stimulus
necessary to produce its action.

2. This golden harvest finds its way into the pockets of those highly-gifted individuals who have acquired the happy knack of writing, or mouthing and spouting, those facetious words, or of performing those grotesque actions, which have the magical power of contracting our cheeks into wrinkles, and distending our jugular veins.

3. All our comic and farcical writers, from Wycherly, Farquhar, Smollett, and the like, down to *Punch*, *Fun*, and *Figaro*, have realised princely incomes by their successful efforts in stimulating the pectoral muscles and shaking the diaphragms of their numerous readers.

4. All our clowns and buffoons and comic singers have found out a most effectual method of "raising the wind" simply by "raising a laugh."

5. The inhabitants of London alone

spend many thousands of pounds annually to support in ease and elegance those dexterous and ingenious eccentrics whose only business it is to make their auditors or spectators laugh.

6. *In former times* to keep *one* fool to provoke laughter was considered so choice a luxury as only to be indulged in by a king. *At the present time* the common people can afford to keep some *hundreds.*

7. Whereas formerly it was regarded as a rare luxury, it is now looked upon as an absolute necessary of life. Witness the multiplicity of our hebdominal facetiæ; witness our Alhambras, our Oxfords, and a thousand other similar *rendezvous* of inferior notoriety, the managers of which are eagerly striving to rival and eclipse each other in their efforts to screw the nerves of their audiences up to the laughing pitch.

8. He who excites the greatest amount of laughter in a given time, either by his pen, his pencil, his tongue, or his grimaces and buffoonery, is considered the reigning favourite *pro tem.*; he is greeted with the loudest plaudits, and, what is of still more importance to him, he receives the greatest pecuniary reward.

9. Indeed, laughter is generally thought to be *so* natural, *so* cheerful, *so* convivial, *so* exhilarating, nay, even *so* healthy, that the monitorial proverb of " laugh and grow fat" has become as " familiar in our mouths as household words."

CHAPTER II.

First—On the organs involved in the action of
laughter. *Second*—On the means by which the
habit of laughing is induced. *Third*—On the
state of feeling to which it gives rise.

1. WHAT is the physical mechanism by
which this remarkable convulsion is gene-
rated? What are the organs by which the
phenomenon of laughter is produced? And
by what stimuli or agency are they put into
motion?

2. One of the older anatomists, in a
Treatise, " De Risa," gives the following
account of the mechanism of laughter :—

3. " No animal," says he, " except man,
is so capable of being tickled, which is occa-

sioned by their not having the papillæ of the nerves so exposed as they are in the human species, in whom these papillæ lie very superficially, especially about the sides of the chest. As these nerves communicate with the nerves which give motion to the muscles of breathing, whenever they are irritated by being tickled, their vibrations are propagated to the communicating nerves, which throws the muscles of breathing into short, quick, and convulsive motions, which is the action of laughter."

4. Now it cannot fail to have been observed—and that repeatedly—by all those who are not absolutely blind, or mentally deficient, that the operation of tickling is invariably commenced at a very early period of infancy, and children are thus taught and accustomed to laugh even before they have begun to think.

5. Thus they learn to laugh, not because they like it, or because they are pleased, but solely because they are tickled; and the association of tickling and laughing is so intimate, and so instantaneous, that children actually begin to laugh even when they merely see the hand of another approaching with the apparent intention of tickling them.

6. Moreover, we may remark, *en passant*, that there are very many habits of an evil and injurious tendency to which children are introduced so gradually, so imperceptibly, and at so very early an age, that the means by which these habits have been formed are altogether overlooked or forgotten, and the habits are regarded, by the superficial and unreflecting, as being perfectly natural and original instincts.

7. Moreover, from the circumstance of their having been acquired so very early in

life, they become, in most cases, fixed and
inveterate.   Such is the case with the habit
of laughing.

8. When we arrive at a capacity of reflecting upon our sensations we perceive, in
the operation of laughter, a ridiculous and
absurd kind of feeling, which we find it
difficult to refer to the class of either pleasure or pain.

9. It may fairly be described as an
amphibious sort of sensation, a vague inde-
finite state of tantalising pleasure in the
very act of transforming itself into a state
of painful annoyance, and from which we
use our utmost endeavours to extricate ourselves as quickly as possible.

10. It is very questionable that children
would ever begin to laugh if they were not
stimulated or prompted, but were let alone,
and treated naturally and rationally.

CHAPTER III.

Further observations on the means employed to
produce what is termed laughter in infants,
and on the injurious effects which result there-
from.

1. IT will be perfectly manifest to any
one who will patiently and carefully and
perseveringly make the requisite observations that infants never do exhibit those
gaspings of breath, accompanied by the compulsory and convulsive ejaculations, which we
complaisantly term laughter, and which we
fondly imagine are the voluntary expressions
of pleasure, except at the instigation of the
nurse or the parent, who jostles or jerks them
about, or squeezes them or tickles them, or

suddenly places some glaring or striking object before them, or some one jumps about, making grotesque or ridiculous motions, or abrupt or shrill noises, all of which annoyances are incessantly inflicted upon the great majority of helpless little infants.

2. These absurd. and preposterous antics very naturally startle and frighten the little vacant-minded creatures, and excite the diaphragm and pectoral muscles into spasmodic action, the result of which is convulsive gaspings for breath.

3. These gaspings for breath gradually become more energetic and vocal, and ultimately result in those reiterated and continued jerkings and heavings of the chest which the parents and nurses foolishly imagine to be manifestations of pleasure and delight, but which, in fact, are nothing more nor less than spasmodic and involuntary con-

A Mother with her Child in her Arms and its Big Sister giggling at it
and tickling it to make it laugh.

Loquitur, Fond Mother (Scotticé Daft Mither)—" When will my
darling ducky begin to laugh ?" Big Sister—" Oh, I'll teach him to
laugh—I'll tickle his little ribs for him, and then he'll soon begin to
laugh! Won't you, baby dear ?"

tractions and dilatations of the pectoral muscles and the lungs, excited into action by those absurd ticklings and stupid monkey tricks which have just been enumerated. (See Engraving.)

4. These irrational pranks by mothers and nurses are practised so frequently and so persistently, and are so invariably and instantaneously followed by the same spasmodic action of the diaphragm and lungs, that the association of these very foolish and vulgar tricks with the immediate agitation of the breathing apparatus ultimately becomes a fixed and permanent association, and continues to influence the manners of most individuals through the whole course of their lives.

5. Furthermore, these absurd and ·stupid excitements are not only unnecessary and vulgar, they are positively mischievous, pro-

ducing effects which are invariably injurious, and sometimes fatal.

6. If these fantastic and insane antics were never practised upon infants, it is morally certain that they would never acquire that tendency to those convulsive twitchings which we denominate laughter, and which, doubtless, in innumerable instances, bring on those convulsive fits which children are so subject to, and which, not unfrequently, end in death.

7. Those fits of laughter which are commonly called *hearty* (but which might more appropriately be termed *violent*) are always constrained, never spontaneous.

8. Fits of laughter never put the body into a pleasant or comfortable state, and we invariably endeavour to put a stop to a fit of laughter as speedily as possible.

9. Coughing is a convulsion somewhat

allied to laughing; they seem to be two species of the same genus: a fit of laughing frequently terminates in a fit of coughing.

10. The physiological fact is that coughing and laughing are both performed by the same important organs, and they both have a very similar influence on the lungs and brain, and that influence is always of a painful and injurious character.

CHAPTER IV.

On the distinction between voluntary actions and those that are involuntary, with a reference to the organs which are employed to produce them.

1. To enable us more clearly to understand the nature and operation of the phenomenon of laughter, let us briefly refer to the well-known fact that some actions are voluntary, while others are involuntary. Our present investigation requires that we should carefully distinguish the different natures of those two species of action.

2. For example, speaking and walking are voluntary actions. We can walk when

we feel inclined, and we can talk when we desire to do so.

3. But sneezing is an involuntary act, as also is coughing; and so is any kind of convulsion. Breathing is likewise an involuntary act, and this function is performed by means of the pectoral muscles and the diaphragm, which are regularly stimulated by the atmospheric air which passes down the trachea into the lungs.

4. Now if we observe the very commencement of those actions which are universally acknowledged to be natural and voluntary, we find that they never require any artificial or external stimulus to induce or provoke their manifestations.

5. For instance, all healthy children have a natural and instinctive tendency to move their arms and legs, and to kick and sprawl about in every possible direction, quite

spontaneously, and without any instigation
or external prompting whatever.

6. In like manner, their vocal organs are
naturally prone to action, and thus they
begin to utter their first simple articulations
of "mamma," "babba," and other similar
elementary sounds, and these operations are
performed (as we may readily observe) quite
spontaneously, and without any extraneous
impulse.

7. Now, everybody knows that the legs
and arms, as well as the vocal organs, belong
to the voluntary system, or that system of
organs which is under the influence of the
will.

8. But the diaphragm and the pectoral
muscles (which, besides being the organs
connected with the essential function of
breathing, are likewise the organs which are
concerned in producing laughter) are not

voluntary, but only act involuntarily from the natural stimulus of the atmosphere upon the lungs, the result of which is respiration.

9. It is extremely improbable (indeed, almost impossible) that these involuntary organs—namely, the pectoral muscles and the diaphragm—would start into convulsion (which they assuredly do in the act of laughing) unless they were acted upon by an unnatural and improper stimulus.

CHAPTER V.

Descriptive of the physical effects of laughter on
the organs of respiration.

1. IN the paroxysm of laughter the lungs
are dilated, and so they remain till the
cause ceases. But while the fit of laughter
continues the blood cannot be transmitted
freely and naturally through the lungs.

2. Hence we can readily account for the
redness and swelling of the neck, face, and
head during a fit of laughter. The blood,
not being allowed to pursue its course through
the lungs, is unnaturally and dangerously
retarded in the veins and arteries, and thus
causes the redness in the neck, face, and
head.

3. If the passage through the lungs be impeded for more than a few seconds the brain becomes congested, apoplexy ensues, and in very many cases ends fatally.

4. Numerous instances are on record in which violent straining and fits of coughing, which have been attended with a full and long-continued inspiration, have terminated in the same fatal manner.

CHAPTER VI.

Is it a confirmed fact (as is universally asserted)
that laughter is an original instinct?   In other
words, Is man really a laughing animal?

1. HAVING briefly described the anatomy
and physiology of laughter, and its patho-
logical action, let us now inquire if universal
experience can be brought forward to prove
that mankind are naturally stimulated to
laugh.

2. It has been affirmed ten thousand times,
and is, moreover, firmly and universally
believed, that man is naturally a laughing
animal, and that it is one of his original and
peculiar instincts to laugh.

3. Upon a mature consideration, however, this assertion appears to be very doubtful.

4. It is certainly a fact that this notion has always prevailed, and its truth has always been taken for granted: no one has even questioned it; consequently, no evidence has ever been set forth in its defence.

5. The bold assertion has gone forth that man is a laughing animal, and straightway, in all ages, it has received the most popular sanction.

6. Nevertheless it still remains an open question, and we are now in a position to state that many facts and arguments are ready to be marshalled in order to show that the only foundations upon which this inveterate opinion has been so long supported, are popular ignorance and that childish credulity which is ever the handmaid of ignorance.

7. Anatomical and physiological facts
have already been adduced to show that
laughter is not the spontaneous and instinctive function of the organs which are
engaged to produce it, and that they must
be stimulated by some influence, which,
obviously, is neither rational nor grateful.

8. Moreover, the following enumeration
of facts will, we feel confident, satisfactorily
prove that the habit of laughing is by no
means universal among mankind. It is
extremely important to keep this in view.

9. For if the act of laughing were truly
one of man's natural functions, it *would* be
universal : all the inhabitants of every country, whether savage or civilised, would invariably exercise the faculty.

10. We at once acknowledge the obvious
fact that an immense number of human
beings *do* laugh, but these are principally

restricted to those countries where what is called civilisation has made considerable progress—where vice and dissipation and all manner of crime abound; and, above all, where levity and frivolity, and every species of folly, constitute the predominant characteristics of the inhabitants, as in England at the present day, to a very great extent, and in France to a very much greater.

11. In such communities the habit of laughing is very prevalent, but it is by no means universal even in those countries.

12. On the other hand it is equally true that in all *un*civilised tribes, among whom vice and crime are comparatively rare— where levity and frivolity are never seen, and where the manners of the people are simple and unsophisticated—in such communities laughter may be said to be entirely unknown.

13. The mothers among these savage tribes never descend to the excessive puerility of tickling or otherwise stimulating their children during infancy. They have no follies, or absurdities, or vices to laugh at—consequently they never laugh.

14. Look at the North American Indians, especially before they were contaminated by intercourse with Europeans, and when their only crime was that of war, which they practised in common with the inhabitants of all civilised and Christian nations.

15. By the united testimony of those Europeans who have travelled among them we learn that the North American Indians never discompose their features by laughter; and this has been corroborated by the writer's personal experience.

16. They naturally preserve a stoical and unvarying equanimity. They neither laugh

nor cry. They are imperturbable under every vicissitude. These are the true and genuine characteristics of the uncivilised North American Indians.

17. In an interesting and very important little book, entitled *Shut Your Mouth*, written by George Catlin, who travelled for many years among those Indians, he makes the following remarks :—" Civilised people, who from their education are more excitable, regarding amusing or alarming scenes with the mouth open, as in wonder, astonishment, delight, listening, &c. ; and in laughing, drawing pleasure through their teeth, by which they insure pain for themselves in their sober moments, and for their teeth diseases of decay which no dentist can cure.

" The savage, without the change of a muscle on his face, listens to the rumbling of the earthquake, or the thunder's crash, with his hand over his mouth ; and if by the extreme of any other excitement he is forced to laugh, his mouth is invariably hidden in the same manner."

18. Here we must observe that what is said to be an Indian's laugh is a mere ejaculation, or sudden emission of breath, and exhibits no similarity to the laugh of the European. The Indian smiles, but he never laughs, according to the meaning of that term as understood among civilised people.

19. Again, if we visit the Southern Hemisphere, and direct our attention to the New Zealanders, we find the same remarks are equally applicable to those aborigines. They had not, when first discovered by early navigators, acquired the habit of spasmodically agitating the diaphragm, and thereby

distorting the countenance with hideous wrinkles.

20. Nevertheless, it cannot be denied that both the North American Indians and the New Zealanders are well-organised human beings, and possess considerable intellectual powers.

21. Among civilised nations, also, there are several who have not yet entered into the laughing stage of humanity.

22. The Hindoos and Arabs are highly intellectual races, yet laughing is an accomplishment which has never been cultivated among them.

23. The Egyptians, the Turks, and the Spaniards are by no means prone to the exercise of risible muscles.

24. Among the ancient Greeks and Romans laughing was not regarded either as dignified or graceful.

25. The wit of their poets and satirists was both acute and refined, exciting admiration and pleasure, but very rarely had the effect of throwing their respiratory apparatus into convulsions.

CHAPTER VII.

On the relation of laughter to wit.

1. GEORGE COMBE (in his *System of Phrenology*), in describing wit, observes :—

" There may be much excellent wit without exciting us to laugh. Indeed, Lord Chesterfield lays it down as a characteristic feature of an accomplished gentleman that *he should never laugh.*

2. It is quite certain that there may be a high enjoyment of wit without laughter.

3. The following are instances in point :—

4. There is a story of a Nottingham publican, whose name was Littlejohn, who put up the figure of Robin Hood for a sign with the following inscription :—

> " All ye that relish ale that's good
> Come in and drink with Robin Hood;
> If Robin Hood is not at home,
> Come in and drink with Little John."

5. This is genuine wit, which even Chesterfield would allow to be so ; and yet it does not force us to laugh.

6. Another instance is the following :—

7. Louis the Fifteenth once heard that an Englishman (Lord Stair) at his court was remarkably like himself.

8. Upon his going to court, the king, who was very guilty of saying rude things, observed, upon seeing him—" A remarkable likeness, upon my word. My Lord, was your mother ever in France ?"

9. To which his lordship replied, with great politeness—" No, please your majesty, but my father was."

10. This was admirably witty, but it does not excite laughter.

11. Again: in the following instance the risible muscles are affected, although, in fact, the real point of wit contained in it is infinitely less.

12. The story of the Nottingham publican, named Littlejohn, who set up the sign of Robin Hood, goes on to say that Mr. Littlejohn having died, his successor thought it a pity to lose so capital a sign and so much good poetry, and accordingly retained them both, only, erasing his predecessor's name, he substituted his own instead.

13. The lines then ran thus :—

> " All ye that relish ale that's good,
> Come in and drink with Robin Hood ;
> If Robin Hood is not at home,
> Come in and drink with Samuel Johnson."

14. The whole wit is now gone, and yet it irresistibly excites laughter.

15. In fact, the ideas have lost all co-

herence, and the wit has been transmuted into a limping, incongruous doggrel. It has become simply ridiculous—hence a subject for laughter.

CHAPTER VIII.

On the logical relation of the action of laughter to the ideas, objects, or actions which excite laughter.

1. I**ᴘ** laughter were instinctive, and consequently natural, there would doubtless be a natural and obvious relation between the laughter and the object or action which gives rise to the laugh, on the well-understood relation which subsists between cause and effect.

2. That is to say, the laugh should have an appropriate and rational relation to the object or action at which we laugh.

3. *We ought to be able to give a good and*

proper reason why we laugh.   QUID RIDES?
should receive a rational response.

4. For instance, let us suppose a frolic-
some young gentleman (a regular practical
joker) showing off his dexterity by suddenly
removing a chair from behind us, just as we
are on the point of sitting down; the
inevitable result is that we come to the floor
with no very pleasant sensations.

5. The silly portion of the company
(which is rarely less than three-fourths)
will think it capital fun, and will exhibit
their delight by a giggle or a grin.

6. Now let us ask—most respectfully—is
there really any consistent relation between
this unfeeling and dangerous joke and the
laugh which immediately follows?

7. Again: it is unfortunately but too
well known that old age deprives many of
us of the natural covering of the scalp, so

that some of us deem it necessary and con-
venient to mount a wig.

8. Under these circumstances it sometimes happens, on a windy day, that the hat
and wig are unceremoniously dismounted,
and begin to perform irregular and most
eccentric gyrations on the pavement.

9. The owner, of course, uses his best
endeavours to regain his fleeting property,
and he is immediately saluted with the obstreperous merriment of the fools who are
passing along.

10. Again let us ask, what necessary
connection can there be discovered between
this annoying accident and the fool's
laugh ?

11. We cannot refrain from adding
another illustration.

12. There is a practice which is very
prevalent among both the ignorant and

intelligent vulgar of retailing low and indecent anecdotes, and immodest witticisms, which are immediately followed by stentorian laughter.

13. We ask once more, is there any natural or rational relation between an obscene joke and a fit of laughter ?

14. Ought it not rather to call forth a frown of indignation or the blush of shame ?

15. The fact is, there is no rational or natural relation (as of cause and effect) between the action of laughter and the action or words at which we laugh.

16. The conclusion is unavoidable, that the absurd habit of laughing is entirely occasioned by the unnatural and false associations which have been forced upon us in early life.

CHAPTER IX.

On the criterion by which to distinguish natural or instinctive actions and habits from those which are acquired.

1. HUNGER and thirst, eating and drinking, talking and walking, fatigue and repose, are all natural, and these actions and sensations are common and universal; they are essential to all healthy and properly organised human beings in every nation in the world; there are no deviations from this natural arrangement.

2. That is to say, the actions of walking and talking, eating and drinking, are invariably performed by every healthy member of the human family, in every country, savage

or civilised; and hunger and thirst, fatigue and repose, are invariably experienced by all.

3. In the performance of such actions as are really natural and instinctive there are no exceptions, either national or individual.

4. Whatever is inherent and natural is essential to the constitution of human beings, and therefore universal.

5. But most decidedly this is not the case with respect to those convulsions which are denominated laughter.

6. All the inhabitants of every country do *not* involuntarily and violently heave their chests and distort their countenances when they witness monkey tricks and buffoonery, or when their ears are assailed by vulgar tales and lewd anecdotes.

CHAPTER X.

On the intellectual and moral status of the ordinary
incentives to laughter.

1. THE remarks in the preceding chapter
naturally lead us to a consideration of the
moral phase of our theme, which undoubtedly presents the most important view
of this novel and interesting question.

2. Let us briefly inquire, in the first
place, what are the objects, the words, and
the actions which excite laughter?

3. And secondly, what are the moral and
intellectual characteristics of those who are
addicted to laughing?

4. The answers to these two questions

will throw considerable light upon our investigation.

5. Now, if we can make it obvious that the words and actions which provoke laughter are neither elevating, nor refining, nor humanising, and that they are incapable of developing or strengthening any one human virtue, we thereby incontestably prove such words and actions are not worthy to be practised or cultivated—that they are, in fact, altogether unworthy of our attention.

6. But if we can still further show that the words and actions which excite laughter are either immoral in their tendency or degrading and vulgarising, we thereby incontestably prove that such words and actions are not only *unworthy* of our attention, but that they ought to be studiously avoided, and that we ought to struggle against them, and, as far as possible, expunge them for

ever from the catalogue of human words and actions.

7. In the first place, then, what are the words and actions which excite laughter?

8. Are they not the absurd, the ridiculous, the mischievous, the wicked, the lewd, the profane?

9. Are they not words and actions which give pain to others?

10. Words and actions which injure the character of others?

11. Words and actions which cause shame and confusion of face to the innocent and virtuous?

12. Smart swindling is laughed at; the exploits of a clever pickpocket raise a laugh; adroit or expert overreaching and cheating in business are choice subjects for laughter.

13. Vicious tricks, practical jokes, and

extravagant and outrageous follies excite laughter.

14. The boisterous and violent demeanour of a drunkard invariably provokes laughter in the superficial and unthinking, and unfortunately the superficial and unthinking constitute ninety-nine in every hundred.

15. The least objectionable causes of laughter are by no means worthy of our imitation or applause—namely, such as are excited by frivolity and nonsense—*fun*, as it is complaisantly called, silly conceits, incongruities, and inconsistencies, which are altogether beneath the self-regard of a sensible man to imitate or encourage.

16. In the mildest terms that can be applied to them they are simply ridiculous and absurd, and certainly indicate a partial suspension of intellect or judgment, an emptiness of mind verging on imbecility.

CHAPTER XI.

On the moral and intellectual characteristics of
those who are addicted to laughing.

1. HABITUAL laughers are invariably
either ignorant, vulgar, or uncultivated.

2. Silly, giddy, frivolous, superficial,
shallow-brained people always laugh im-
moderately at the merest trifles; and extremely empty-headed simpletons acquire
such an inveterate habit of laughing, that
they involuntarily laugh at absolutely
nothing.

3. What is the most striking peculiarity
of the mockers, the gibers, the taunters, the
scoffers?

E

4. Are they not invariably the inveterate laughers?

5. Are they not, in general, the coarse, the vulgar, the brutal, the unfeeling?

6. What are the feelings of those who are laughed at? Who likes to be laughed at?

7. Children (who, of course, are ignorant) laugh considerably—that is to say, in civilised countries.

8. As they grow older, and gain knowledge and good sense, their laughing propensity gradually becomes weaker, and the habit of laughing gradually diminishes.

9. If they become studious and intelligent (which all human beings ought to become) the spasm of laughter is rarely exhibited.

10. The author of the following lines (which constitute the *refrain* of a Bacchanalian lyric) very candidly sets forth the close and

intimate relation which subsists between folly and laughter :—

> " Francs buveurs qui Bacchus attire
> Dans ses retraites qu'il cherit,
> Avec nous, venez *boire* et *rire*—
> Plus on est de *foux*—plus on *rit.*"

11. In general terms we may assert (and it will, doubtless, accord with the experience of all those who observe and reflect) that ignorant, frivolous fools are almost continually on the giggle or titter, whilst intelligent and sensible people (whose thoughts are, of course, occupied with good and useful ideas) seldom descend to laughter.

12. Indeed, if a man's mind be occupied by good and useful ideas, how can it be possible for him to laugh?

CHAPTER XII.

Are laughter and joking, badinage and fun, consistent with dignity of character ? or are they
conducive to the maintenance of a beneficial
political or social influence ?

1. THE following observations, which appeared in the *Daily Telegraph* of September,
1868 (although written *en badinage*), are
true to the letter, and exhibit an excellent
illustration of the correctness of the theory
which we have had the hardihood to espouse
and defend in the preceding pages :—

2. "It is," says the writer "rather a loss
to Mr. Osborne (who is fighting hard for his
seat at Nottingham) that he is not a dull

man. If he makes a really clever sug-
gestive speech, it is sure to be besprinkled
with jokes—so broken up by 'laughter' in
parenthesis, that the graver parts are apt to
be passed over by the many readers who
detest to be instructed, and who like to be
amused.

3. "An Osborne without his jokes would
be a fair statesman of the second rank, and
far superior to the average intellect of the
twelve or thirteen that go to form the rank
and file of a Conservative Cabinet. His
intellect is as clear, his ability of exposition
as great, his acuteness in detecting fallacies
as keen, as that of any speaker in either
House.

4. "But Englishmen are much attached
to grave men.

5. "The late Sir Robert Peel had, we be-
lieve, a deep sense of humour in private

society, but in public life he was pre-eminently a grave man ; and he owed a great deal of the reverence felt for him, even by his opponents, to the solemnity of his manner and the steady seriousness of his tone.

6. "The Earl of Chatham was grave, and he retained his influence even when his mistakes were as grave as himself.

7. "Pitt was solemn.

8. "Lord Grey was always dignified, decorous, and incapable of a joke ; and in such men a popular confidence is placed which is seldom or never given to men of wit and humour about town.

9. "Fox lost caste, because, though his policies were wise, and would have saved us millions of our debt, he was light-hearted and gay.

10. "In his own day Canning was successfully attacked because he was a joker of

jokes, and spiteful antagonists denied his statesmanship because he had penned witty lampoons.

11. "Lord Melbourne, who really had the instincts of a true statesman, was always underrated; and Palmerston had to live down, for forty years, the effects of his *bonhommie* and his readiness to jest.

12. "In fact, our national character is mainly grave; Englishmen may laugh at jokes, but they distrust the joker.

13. "Sidney Smith was one of the ablest preachers whom the English Church had produced for generations; a conscientious pastor and a thorough Churchman, he stood in the foreground, fighting the battles of liberality and religious truth when there was no chance of any earthly reward; yet the Liberals passed him over, and appointed to bishoprics utterly inferior men, simply

because he was humorous and witty, and they were irredeemably grave.

14. "We should therefore be inclined to advise Mr. Osborne to mend his ways. Let him abjure jokes. Let him never provoke 'laughter.' Let him be bigoted, solemn, and dull, and he will be made a Tory minister; or let him be statistical and serious, and he may one day get an Under-Secretaryship from a Liberal Ministry."

15. We consider it no exaggeration to declare this article to be as clever and as truthful a sketch as ever appeared in the columns of the *Daily Telegraph*.

CHAPTER XIII.

The verdict of Shakspeare on the moral character
of laughter.

1. ALTHOUGH our Immortal Bard has not
founded any of his dramatic works or poems
expressly on the theme of laughter, he has,
nevertheless, expressed himself in very
explicit and energetic terms in favour of the
opinions and views which it has been the
object of these pages to expound.

2. In the dialogue between Biron and
Rosaline (in *Love's Labour Lost*) he has thus
unfolded his ideas on the subject :—

BIRON *to* ROSALINE. Impose some service on me
for thy love.

RosALINE.   Oft have I heard of you, my Lord
    Biron,
Before I saw you, and the world's large tongue
Proclaims you for a man replete with mocks,
Full of comparisons and wounding flouts,
Which you on all estates will execute
That lie within the mercy of your wit.
To weed this wormwood from your fruitful brain,
And therewithal to win me, if you please
(Without the which I am not to be won),
You shall, this twelvemonth term, from day to day,
Visit the speechless sick, and still converse
With groaning wretches; and your task shall be,
With all the fierce endeavour of your wit,
To enforce the painèd impotents to smile.
   BIRON.   To move wild laughter in the throat of
    death?
It cannot be—it is impossible.
   RosALINE.   Why that's the way to choke a gibing
    spirit,
Whose influence is begot of that loose grace
Which shallow laughing hearers give to fools.
A jest's prosperity lies in the ear
Of him that hears it—never in the tongue
Of him that makes it.   Then, if sickly ears,

Deaf'd with the clamour of their own dear groans,
Will hear your idle scorns—continue then,
And I will have you, and that fault withal.
But if they will not—throw away that gibing spirit,
And I shall find you empty of that fault,
Right joyful of your reformation.

3. We most earnestly request the reader to direct his particular and deliberate attention to this passage from Shakspeare.

4. A clearer or more convincing demonstration of the correctness of our theory could not possibly be set forth than the poet has presented in this exquisite episode.

5. There are many actions and incidents, ideas and recitals, which are relished and laughed at by the giddy, the ignorant, and the unreflecting, but which, on the contrary, excite the indignation and disgust of the intelligent and humane.

6. The wise, the prudent, and the thoughtful rarely laugh.

7. The more we improve ourselves, the more we cultivate and refine our manners and conversation, the more efforts we make to be useful, and the more we strive to do good, just in the same degree we cease to be agitated by the convulsions and distortions of laughter.

8. The natural and certain result of such a course of intellectual and moral progress would be, that we should live a higher life, consequently experience a more perfect state of happiness; and this is, or ought to be,

"Our being's end and aim."

CHAPTER XIV.

A brief comparison between gravity and levity—
The grave and the gay—Have we any rule to
direct us in the exercise of laughter?

1. WHEN we compare the moral attributes
of gravity with those of levity, or seriousness with frivolity, we can hardly avoid the
conclusion that they bear nearly the same
relation to each other as virtue bears to vice,
or wisdom to folly.

2. Gravity and seriousness always exert a
beneficial influence, whereas frivolity and
levity, on the contrary, produce a demoralis-
ing and vulgarising effect.

3. Gravity and decorum are the striking
characteristics of the wise and prudent—

frivolity and laughter are the predominating features of ignorance and folly.

4. Moreover, there is no consistent principle or fixed standard by which a person may be guided in the use of laughter.

5. Superficial fools and ignorant boors will laugh vociferously at that which would only excite contempt in the mind of an educated man.

6. Conversely, there are many sayings and doings which an intelligent man would appreciate as genuine wit, but at which the shallow-brained ignoramus would listen and gape with a vacant stare.

7. The prevalence of folly and vice will produce very different effects on the opposite temperaments of the grave and the gay.

8. Heraclitus wept at the follies, frivolities, and vicissitudes of human existence Democritus laughed at them.

CHAPTER XV.

On the degrading and vicious consequences of the
habit of laughing.

1. In· the present chapter we shall
endeavour to point out that the obstreperous
and meaningless habit of laughing is, if not
the entire cause, at least one of the principal
causes, of the existence and continuance of
the follies, frivolities, mischiefs, and lewd
conversations which are now so rampant in
every class of society, and which sink it so
low in the moral scale.

2. The actors of all practical jokes, the
authors of every species of mischief, the
retailers of low, vulgar, and obscene

anecdotes, together with utterers of scandal, are all instigated by the very contemptible ambition of raising a laugh, a giggle, or a smirk at some one's expense.

3. These miserable mongers of foul talk, and these vulgar performers of practical jokes, exhibit their absurd antics, and retail their obscene anecdotes, for the express purpose of exciting laughter, which they expect and look for as a gratification and reward for their ingenuity, dexterity, or wit.

4. This being the case, we may safely conclude that if follies, vulgarities, and absurdities were never laughed at, but were listened to in silence, and treated with the contempt which they really deserve, they would soon cease to be practised.

5. Who would transform themselves into monkeys, or magpies, or buffoons (as thousands are in the habit of doing), if their un-

meaning absurdities were visited with silence and contempt?

6. Who would continue to indulge in gibes and mocks and ribaldry, or shameless conversation, if they were received with a frown or a rebuke?

7. All these abominations and annoyances are continued, and actually expand and increase, precisely because they are incessantly laughed-at.

8. Not only are absurdities, and follies, and mischiefs supported and perpetuated by being rewarded with a vulgar laugh, but very many vices and actual crimes are regarded by the volatile and unreflecting as capital jokes, and are greeted with a hearty burst of laughter.

9. Thomas Carlyle says that England contains twenty millions of people, mostly

fools.   We cannot help fully endorsing
Carlyle's estimate.

10. That there are so many fools is
mainly to be attributed to the false and
absurd associations which are engrafted upon
the minds of human beings during the
pliant period of infancy and childhood, and
more especially to those most ridiculous
associations which are connected with the
mindless habit of laughing.

CHAPTER XVI.

On the injurious effects of nursery rhymes and
juvenile literature in stultifying the minds of
children and youths by furnishing them with
extravagant lies and egregious nonsense to
excite their wonder and induce them to laugh.

1. With very few exceptions the books
composed expressly for children have always
been, and still continue to be, of the most
trashy description, and have had a powerful
and marked effect in degrading the morals
and stultifying the intellect.

2. They are generally made up of the
veriest nonsense and the most monstrous
absurdities.

3. These burlesque productions are chiefly

designed to amuse by arousing the wonder of their vacant-minded readers, by the relation of the most ridiculous and outrageous lies, and to excite their laughter by the recital of the most grotesque actions, and the grossest follies and ribaldry.

4. In order to verify the correctness of this somewhat severe criticism nothing more will be necessary than to enumerate a few of the titles of these gems of fiction, these pure efforts of the imagination—to wit :—*Jack the Giant-Killer, Jack and the Bean-Stalk, Hop o' my Thumb, Seven League Boots, Old Mother Hubbard, Puss in Boots, Goody Two Shoes, Little Red Riding Hood.*

5. We might easily append (if it were requisite) the names of a host of more modern productions of an equally interesting and edifying description, adorned with elaborate works of art, exhibiting the skill and ingenuity

of the artist in supplementing the heathen mythology by the addition of such hideous monsters as had never been dreamt of in the wildest dreams of the poets and sculptors of remote antiquity.

6. Can we wonder at the immense number of silly, frivolous, giddy, giggling, full-grown fools, who, in the present reign of Queen Victoria, infest all ranks of society, when we reflect that their nascent minds were perverted, and distorted, and shrivelled in their infancy and childhood by such surpassing nonsense and trashy garbage as the nursery rhymes and juvenile literature we have just described, and which are not only permitted, but universally encouraged ?

7. These extremely stupid and vulgar books have been, and still continue to be, the bane and curse of the intellect of the rising

generation, and, in a vast majority of cases, the utter ruin of their morals.

8. Nor can we hope to have any improvement in the conduct and conversation of human beings until our present nursery literature shall be completely swept away, and replaced by books of a pure and rational character.

CHAPTER XVII.

A venial digression touching the false and imperfect methods now in vogue of teaching and training the young.

1. It cannot be denied that our present methods of training young children are lamentably deficient; many of them, indeed, are altogether contrary to reason.

2. For instance, it is perfectly well known that whatever we teach children which is of a sensible or useful character we impose it upon them as a task; but in their leisure hours they are not only allowed, but encouraged, to relax their moral principles and effeminate their intellects by reading the

most incredible romances and story-books;
to amuse themselves with irrational and
antagonistic games, and to fill up the inter-
vals with rude idle talk.

3. Moreover, the generality of parents and
nurses are continually laughing at, and consequently encouraging, the silly and unmeaning babble and tattle and chatter of
their children.

4. Thus the inexperienced children very
naturally begin to associate the action of
laughter with trashy nonsense and foolish
talk, till it becomes, in a great majority of
cases, the ruling passion and a permanent
habit; and thus they entirely exclude from
the mind the important consideration that
folly and laughter do not, under any circumstances, constitute a part of the duties of
human life.

5. Parents almost universally ignore the

serious responsibility which their thoughtless neglect involves. They entirely forget—although the injunction has been repeatedly laid upon them—"That for every idle word that men shall speak they shall give an account on the day of judgment. For by thy words thou shalt be justified, and by thy words thou shalt be condemned."

6. As actions are of still more importance than words, this sweeping and emphatic denunciation evidently implies the guilt of those who commit idle or ridiculous *actions*, as well as those who utter idle *words*, for the minor in this case obviously includes the major.

7. Everything that we teach children, every book that we put into their hands to read, should have some decided relation to rational ideas or virtuous principles, to some rule of conduct, or to some useful action.

CHAPTER XVIII.

Milton *versus* Shakspeare on the subject of
laughter.

1. WE have already condemned, in no
very measured terms, the current literature
provided for the young by inferior and unknown authors and artists; but the manu-
facturers of nursery rhymes and children's
story-books are not alone responsible for the
moral debasement produced by grossly exciting and contaminating literature.

2. Men of the highest stamp have de-
graded themselves and prostituted their
great talents to the propagation of loose
principles and the encouragement of licen-
tious actions.

3. As a specimen of this unpardonable misapplication of the most splendid endowments take the following extract from *L'Allegro.*

4. It is scarcely necessary to inform the reader that this poem is from the pen of the sublime, the divine, the immortal Milton.

5. The poet is evidently in a revelling mood, and he invites one of the Graces, together with others of a kindred character, that his orgies may reach a climax.

" Come, thou goddess, fair and free,
  In heaven yclept Euphrosyne,
  And, by men, heart-easing Mirth,
  Whom lovely Venus at a birth,
  With two sister Graces more,
  To ivy-crownèd Bacchus bore ;
  Or whether (as some sages say)
  The frolic wind that breathes the spring,
  Zephyr with Aurora playing
  There on beds of violet blue
  And fresh-blown roses washed in dew,

Filled her with thee a daughter fair,
So buxom, blithe, and debonnair.
Haste thee, nymph, and bring with thee,
Jest and youthful jollity,
Quips and cranks and wanton wiles,
Nods and becks and wreathèd smiles,
Such as hang on Phœbe's cheek,
And love to live in dimple sleek.
Sport that wrinkled Care derides,
And Laughter holding both his sides—
Come and trip it as you go,
On the light fantastic toe,
And in thy right hand lead with thee
The mountain nymph, sweet Liberty.
And if I give thee honour due,
Mirth, admit me of thy crew,
To live with her, and live with thee
In unreprovèd pleasures free."

6. Can we imagine a more attractive or more seducing invocation to the indulgence of the grossest, the most vitiating, the most brutifying of all the sensual appetites?

7. Verily, the moral world owes John

Milton (of *Paradise Lost* celebrity) a certain amount of pity—not unmingled with contempt—for setting forth, in such euphonious strains, such alluring incentives to debauchery.

CHAPTER XIX.

A comparison between those sayings and doings which are laughed at and those which are *not* laughed at.

1. A BRIEF summary of the words and actions which we are in the habit of laughing at, compared with those which do not excite laughter, will exhibit the argument in a still morec onvincing form.

2. We laugh at folly, frequently at vice—we never laugh at wisdom, or justice, or any other cardinal virtues.

3. We laugh at practical jokes and mischievous pranks—we never laugh at gratitude, or acts of benevolence, or any species of kindness.

4. We laugh at many species of crime, lewd conversation, and vulgar anecdotes—we never laugh at gentlemanly or honourable conduct, or any species of virtuous or edifying conversation.

5. We frequently laugh at wit, satire, sarcasm. But these are all used to point out or stigmatise something injurious, degrading, dishonourable, or contemptible; something ridiculous, or some incongruity; or to scandalise some one, or to bring some one into contempt, or to castigate some folly or injustice.

6. The vices and failings we have just enumerated are doubtless legitimate objects of laughter and ridicule whenever or wherever they exhibit themselves, *if* by laughter and ridicule they can be gradually put down and finally abolished.

7. For it must be universally acknow-

ledged that all these evil, injurious, and degrading qualities are vices which should have been eradicated in early youth, or rather which should not have been allowed to take root—and then the wit, satire, and sarcasm would not have been required to rebuke them; consequently, the stimulus which they present to excite our risible muscles into action would no longer exist.

8. We laugh at ignorance, but never at intelligence or useful knowledge.

9. We laugh at the caricatures and burlesques — the vulgar witticisms and outrageous nonsense of Beaumont, Fletcher, Fielding, Prior, Butler, and other similar humorists — but we never laugh at the sublime and virtue-inspiring precepts of Pythagoras, Epictetus, Plutarch, or Seneca.

CHAPTER XX.

The character of Laughers compared with the character of those who are thoughtful and serious

1. LET us repeat the fact (which should be continually borne in mind by all those who maintain that laughter is consistent with propriety and decorum)—namely, that habitual laughers are silly, giddy, frivolous, superficial persons—that is to say, they are, in one expressive word—fools.

2. A second fact requires equally to be remembered—namely, that sensible and intelligent persons, whose lives are occupied in the important duties of improving their minds, in being useful, and in doing good,

and whose leisure hours are spent in rational, cheerful, and humanising enjoyments—such persons (male or female) are rarely tempted to laugh ; and many very excellent men and women never laugh under any possible circumstances.

3. The gentle, the most amiable, the most intelligent, the most virtuous are rarely prone to laughter.

4. On the other hand, the worst of characters, the depraved, the dissipated, the criminal are generally much addicted to uproarious mirth and laughter.

5. Moreover (to summarise what we have already stated in detail), all the innumerable words and actions which induce or compel people to laugh are invariably tainted with some degree of folly, vice, or crime—absurdity, stupidity, or nonsense—levity, frivolity, or trifling—all of which, it

must be at once acknowledged, are decidedly objectionable, and should, therefore, as soon as possible, be utterly swept away.

6. An evident and most important corollary may be deduced from the latter proposition—namely, that the more these vices can be avoided and got rid of, the better it will be for the happiness of mankind.

7. Rationality, good sense, wisdom, virtue, righteousness are never laughed at; but these are precisely the qualities which should universally abound.

8. We may very safely conclude that the universal predominance of these qualities would be the total annihilation of laughter.

CHAPTER XXI.

Classification of Laughs and Smiles.

THE following list enumerates a few of the various kinds of laughs and smiles, classified in genera, species, and varieties:—

The first genus is the "Laugh," exhibiting five species, namely—

1. The giggling laugh, excited by romping fun and nonsense.

2. The hearty laugh, instigated by practical jokes or extremely absurd antics.

3. The full-faced laugh of the weaker sex.

4. The boisterous laugh of the stronger sex.

The Benevolent Smile, prompted by Loving-kindness.

5. The *Ne plus ultra* laugh, which may be variously denominated as the obstreperous laugh—the vociferous laugh—the stentorian laugh—or the horse laugh.

The *second* genus is the "Smile," under which we have arranged four species, each containing a certain number of varieties.

First species—Simulated smiles, containing six varieties—namely,

1. The condescending or patronising smile.

2. The insidious smile.

3. The sardonic sneer or furtive leer.

4. The beseeching or persuading smile.

5. The ironical or don't-you-wish-you-may-get-it? smile.

6. The cajoling smirk or wheedling grin.

Second species—Vulgar or unintellectual smiles, containing three varieties—namely,

1. The credulous simper or gullible smile.

2. The chuckle or exulting smile.

3. The vague persistent smile, or vacant simper.

Third species—Refined, intellectual, and amiable smiles, containing ten varieties—namely,

1. The entreating smile of infancy.

2. The confiding smile of childhood.

3. The maternal sympathetic smile.

4. The infant's smile of delight.

5. The grandmother's affectionate smile.

6. The grandchild's grateful smile.

7. The joyous smile of friendly recognition.

8. The supremely affectionate smile.

9. The pensive smile.

10. The self-conceited smile, or smile of self-esteem.

Fourth species — The creature-comfort smiles, containing two varieties—namely,

1. Sawney's snuff-tickling smile.

2. Jack Tar's joyful smile over "the cup that cheers but not inebriates."

The species of laughter are as limited in their range as those of the smile are extensive.

Each individual, when under the influence of laughter, puts forth his or her peculiar giggle, grin, snort, or titter, which generally preserves its identical intonation and ring as long in life as the laughing habit continues, or till old age subdues it.

It would appear that the only variation of which a laugh is susceptible consists in its greater or less degree of intensity.

CHAPTER XXII.

On the broad line of demarcation which separates
laughter from smiling.

1. In discoursing of "Laughter" and
"Smiling," we must carefully guard against
the popular fallacy of confounding these
very distinct modifications of the countenance.

2. These two functions of the fibrous
tissue exhibit very dissimilar species of
action.

3. A laugh is generally regarded as a
smile continued and intensified and carried
out to a climax.

4. When, however, they are carefully

analysed they will be found to be quite distinct—distinct in essence, distinct in origin, distinct in action, distinct in effect; producing and manifesting very dissimilar states of feeling.

5. Walker (in his Dictionary) defines the verb to laugh at—to treat with contempt, to ridicule, to deride, to scorn.

6. The same authority defines the verb to smile—to be favourable, to be propitious, to look with pleasure or kindness.

7. We will endeavour to amplify upon these definitions, and to give an analysis which will more distinctly exhibit the con-trast.

8. A laugh distorts every feature, and renders even a handsome face unpleasing and ridiculous, so that a refined and intelligent spectator is apt to turn away from it.

9. A smile lights up the countenance

with all the radiance of beauty, invests it with an irresistible attraction, and imparts a pleasure which no language can adequately describe.

10. A laugh is invariably accompanied by a convulsive action of the diaphragm.

11. Sir Charles Bell, treating of the phenomenon of Laughter in his celebrated treatise on the "Anatomy of Expression," presents us with the following vivid description:—

12. "Observe the condition of a man convulsed with laughter. He draws a full breath, and throws it out in short, interrupted, and audible cachinnations. The muscles of his throat, neck, and chest are agitated; the diaphragm is especially convulsed. He holds his sides, and from the violent agitation he is incapable of a voluntary act."

13. Although the irresistible convulsion of the diaphragm is the principal of the physical manifestations of laughter, yet there are several accessories, especially the sharp vocal utterances arising from the violent distension of the larynx, and the wrinkled and distorted expression of every feature.

14. A smile is entirely free from all these violent and painful emotions—no convulsions —no distortions—no violent distension of the vocal organs.

15. In laughter the strain upon the muscles concerned in the operation deprives the laugher of the power of exercising any of his other faculties. He can neither think, speak, nor act. As Sir Charles Bell expresses it, "he is incapable of a voluntary act."

16. How exactly the reverse are the manifestations of a *smile*, during which all

the faculties have full scope—the thoughts
are the purest, the words are the gentlest,
the actions are the kindest !

17. A laugh is always accompanied by a
disagreeable noise, which cannot be more
correctly designated than as *idiotic*. It
invariably produces a silly, vulgar, unmeaning sound—whether it be a giggle or a grin
—a compressed he ! he !—an expanded ha !
ha ! or a downright broad horse laugh.

18. A smile never gives rise to the
least noise or sound of any kind ; it manifests
the kindliest sympathies in sweet and
gentle silence.

[The reader must bear in mind that we
are here speaking of the smile of sincerity,
candour, and benevolence—the most essential
characteristics of humanity, properly so
called.

The vicious, the cunning, the overreaching, with flexible features and apt imitative faculties, can easily simulate a smile of any kind or degree.

Hamlet, after the interview with the ghost of his father, takes out his tablets to write a record, saying—

" Villain, villain, *smiling* damned villain—
———————— Meet it is I sat it down
That one may *smile* and *smile* and be a villain."]

19. The various species of laughter are all ridiculous, absurd, or impudent—vulgar or idiotic—presenting ugliness to the sight, and harsh and grating sounds to the ear.

20. The various species of the genuine or amiable smile are all beautiful, whether of benevolence or kindness—sympathy or gratitude—admiration, veneration, or affection—they are all sweetness and beauty.

21. We suspect a laugh, we confide in a smile; contempt and ridicule lurk under a

laugh, love and friendship beam in a smile.

22. Another very marked distinction between smiling and laughing is this :—*Smiling* may be caused—and, in fact, is generally caused—by witnessing the exhibition of any of the virtues; but we cannot imagine, for a moment, the possibility of any sane person *laughing* at the performance of an honourable or virtuous action.

A Series of Engravings

EXHIBITING A FEW SPECIMENS OF THE DIS-
TORTIONS WHICH LAUGHTER PRODUCES ON
THE " HUMAN FACE DIVINE."

The Giggling Laugh, excited by Boisterous Fun and
Nonsense.

The Obstreperous Laugh, instigated by Practical Jokes
or Extreme Absurdities.

The Hearty Laugh of the Gentler Sex.

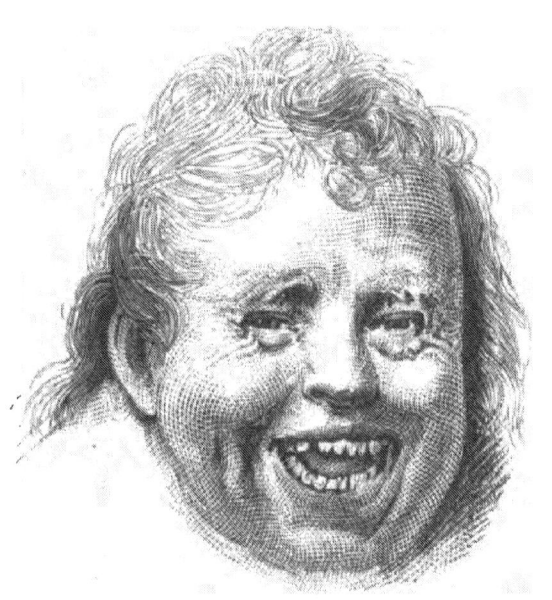

The Stentorian Laugh of the Stronger Sex.

The Superlative Laugh, or Highest Degree of Laughter.

CHAPTER XXIII.

Further illustrations of the distinction between a laugh and a smile.

1. THE thoughtful and curious reader may naturally ask—"Are there any definite and precise criteria by which we can at once truly distinguish a smile from a laugh?"

2. We answer—"Most assuredly there are," and we shall now endeavour to point them out.

3. Whatever may be the exciting cause of laughter, the paroxysm comes on suddenly, shaking the whole bodily frame, particularly the lungs, the diaphragm, and pectoral muscles.

H

The Obstreperous Laugh, instigated by Practical Jokes
or Extreme Absurdities.

10. A smile comes on gently, does not
agitate the breathing apparatus in the least
degree, and subsides as gently as it commenced.

11. Smiling causes no headache or aching
of the sides, nor does it give rise to any
pain or disturbing sensations in any of the
bodily organs.

12. The state of the organism in a fit of
laughter is a state of painful excitement and
agitation, and is, moreover, morally annoying
to any one possessing the least dignity of
character or thoughtful reflection.

13. The continuance of a fit of laughter,
even for a few minutes, would, from the intensity of its convulsions, assuredly prove
fatal.

14. The physical state of the organism
during the manifestation of a smile is perfect tranquillity and repose. The moral

state of consciousness is pleasurable beyond expression.

15. A smile may be continued *ad libitum* for any possible length of time, without causing any other than pleasurable sensations.

16. A smile, as we have already observed, is quite spontaneous, whilst a true laugh is invariably compulsory, and it is often excited in direct opposition to our wishes.

The following illustrations present a few examples of the infinite variety of the smile by which the different emotions or passions of the human soul are made manifest on the countenance.

The Condescending or the Patronising Smile.

The Insidious Smile.

The Sardonic Sneer, or Furtive Leer.

The Beseeching or Persuading Smile.

The Ironical or "Don't-you-wish-you-may-get-it" Smile.

The Cajoling Smirk, or Wheedling Grin.

The Credulous Simper, or the Gullible Smile.

The Chuckle, or Exulting Smile.

The Vague Persistent Smile, or Vacant Simper.

REFINED, INTELLECTUAL, AND AMIABLE

SMILES.

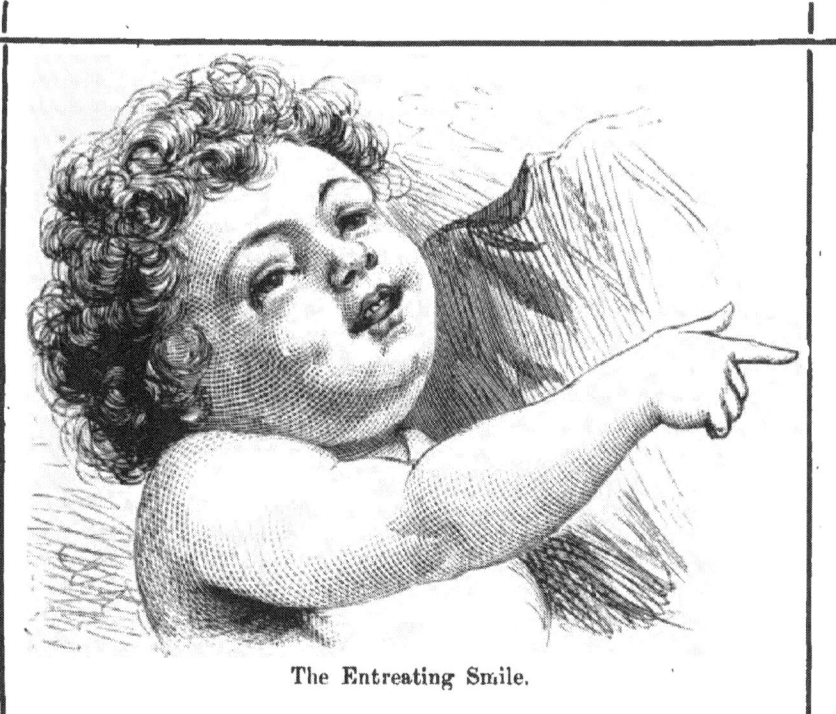

The Entreating Smile.

The Confiding Smile.

The Mother's Sympathetic Smile, and the Infant's
Smile of Delight.

The Grandmother's Affectionate Smile, and the Grandchild's
Grateful Smile.

The Joyous Smile of Friendly Recognition.

The Supremely Affectionate Smile.

The Pensive Smile.

The Self-conceited Smile, or the Smile of Self-Esteem.

Sawney's Snuff-Tickling Smile.

The Joyful Smile over the Cup that Cheers but
not Inebriates.

CHAPTER XXIV.

Is it a fact (as is generally affirmed) that those who are habituated to laugh are good-tempered, generous, and philanthropic? And, on the contrary, that those who seldom or never laug are gloomy, repulsive, and misanthropic characters who ought to be suspected and shunned?

1. NOTIONS and opinions that pass current in society generally gain our belief and confidence without our giving them the least examination.

2. For example :—It has been frequently asserted, with the greatest assurance, that a man who never laughs is morose, unfeeling, malignant, a suspicious character not to be trusted.

3. Like many of our traditional notions, this is purely a popular fallacy.

4. We have only to exercise our powers of observation to become aware of the existence of many instances of individuals who very rarely laugh, and who are, nevertheless, not only highly intellectual, but highly amiable and benevolent.

5. On the other hand, the instances are very numerous of individuals who are very great proficients in the exercise of laughing and giggling, who are nevertheless very slightly endowed with either intellect, amiability, or benevolence.

6. When we call to mind the character and writings of the great and wise men of antiquity, we can hardly conceive them to be jesters, harlequins, or merry-andrews.

7. Imagine, for a moment, of Confucius or Pythagoras reciting jokes to their pupils

to excite a laugh, as many of our orators do at the present day.

8. Can we conceive of Plato wrinkling his features, and distending his jugular veins, in order to amuse his listeners?

9. Did Plutarch set the table in a roar? Did Cicero's orations induce his audiences to shake their sides?

10. When we read Isaiah and the Prophets do we distort our features? Was St. Paul a "man of wit and humour about town?"

11. Whatever the ancient sages may have done in their ignorant and childish days, we cannot resist the conclusion that when they came to years of maturity they were men who never laughed.

12. We read in one verse in the New Testament that "Jesus wept," but there is no record that He ever laughed; nor can we

conceive the probability or consistency of such an event.

13. Thus we perceive that laughter does not make a good man, and that there are thousands of good men who never laugh.

CONCLUDING.

1. HEARKEN to the voice of the wise man. (Eccles. vii. 2—6.) "It is better to go to the house of mourning than to the house of feasting. Sorrow is better than laughter.

2. "The heart of the wise is in the house of mourning, but the heart of fools is in the house of mirth.

3. "It is better to hear the voice of the wise than for a man to hear the song of fools.

4. "For as the crackling of thorns under a pot, so is the laughter of fools."

5. Whatever is good and true, kind and

---

benevolent, whatever is beautiful and good, excellent and useful, whatever is grand and noble, magnificent or magnanimous, never gives rise to the "Madness of Laughter."

6. But these are precisely the qualities which produce human happiness, and there-fore they are the qualities which should universally abound.

7. In proportion as these qualities increase and multiply, so will laughter dwindle and diminish. When these qualities become universal, laughter will expire.

FOUR MODIFICATIONS OF THE SAME COUNTENANCE,

NAMELY,

1st. The natural and usual state of silent thought or calm reflection.

2nd. A gentle smile under the influence of kindly sensations.

3rd. Exhibiting the expression of moderate laughter.

4th. Displaying the influence of hearty laughter.

The four illustrations which follow are engraved from photographs of a lady whom nature and education have so favoured as to place her above the average of her sex both in intellect and accomplishments.

First Portrait.

THE NATURAL AND USUAL STATE OF SILENT
THOUGHT OR CALM REFLECTION.

The first portrait presents the countenance in a state of repose, under the
influence of silent thought and calm

Second Portrait.

A GENTLE SMILE, UNDER THE INFLUENCE OF
KINDLY SENSATIONS.

The second portrait exhibits the features (under the influence of kindly sensations) modified with a smile which may be appropriately termed the *Ingenuous Smile*, happily illustrating the words of the poet—

> " Her mouth, which a smile,
> Devoid of all guile,
>   Half opened to view,
> Is the bud of the rose,
> In the morning that blows,
>   Impearled with the dew.
>   *Old Ballad.*

Third Portrait.

**EXHIBITING THE EXPRESSION OF MODERATE
LAUGHTER.**

The third portrait represents the face during the action of moderate laughter, caused by thoughts, words, or actions of an incongruous, absurd, or ridiculous character. This is invariably accompanied by short jerking emissions of breath, giving rise to a rapid succession of abrupt and involuntary sounds which are neither melodious nor agreeable.

Fourth Portrait.

DISPLAYING THE INFLUENCE OF HEARTY
LAUGHTER.

The fourth portrait displays the influence of a hearty fit of laughter, which is invariably caused by extravagant, outrageous, and egregious nonsense. We go to see the pantomime to enable us to realise this extreme convulsion.

APPENDIX,

COLLATERAL AND EXPLANATORY,

———◆◆◆———

SECTION I.

*On the various species of tickling, physical,
intellectual, and moral.*

1. ALL gentle friction or rubbing of the
body may be classed under the generic term
of tickling, and may be appropriately denominated *physical tickling*.

2. But the mind may be—and can be—
and very frequently is—tickled quite as
effectually as is the physical organism.

3. The intellect is susceptible of being
tickled by ideas, and the moral faculties—in

combination with the intellect—can be tickled on witnessing the representation of certain actions, generally of a vulgar or immoral character.

4. Now it is very well known that every species of physical, intellectual, or moral tickling gives rise—in a greater or less degree—to those convulsive gaspings and wrinkled distortions of the countenance which characterise the phenomenon of laughter.

5. The superficial nervous papillæ are tickled by physical contact of some foreign substance, and then laughter is mechanically induced, entirely without the concurrence or accompaniment of either intellectual perception or moral sensation.

6. The reading or oral recital of the details of any incongruous, absurd, or grotesque transaction, or the recounting of

nonsensical, outrageous, or obscene incidents or anecdotes, will tickle the intellect of those whose intellects are effeminate, stunted, or warped, or have not been properly trained; and the result will be cachinnations of a more or less stentorious character, according to the degree of piquancy in the description or anecdote.

7. Again. The moral faculties of those whose moral faculties are but slightly influenced by any moral principles (and these constitute all but a mere tithe of the community) are stimulated by witnessing the operations of any kind of practical jokes, and then the vociferations of laughter are loud and deep in proportion to the amount of mischief, annoyance, or pain which the practical joke may inflict upon the victim.

8. The intensity of the laughter at practical jokes generally reaches a higher obstre-

perous pitch than the laughter occasioned
by any other stimulus.

9. Now let us seriously ask—what
amount of common sense, what amount of
benevolence, or of any other moral virtue,
can there exist in the minds of those who
are excited into boisterous raptures at the
exhibition of gratuitous mischief or reckless
cruelty ?

SECTION II.

Remarks on the effects of physical tickling.—Quoted
from a French cyclopædia.

1. CHATOUILLEMENT, c'est-à-dire, un at-
touchement particulier qui porte sur la peau
une impression qui fait rire.

2. Mais si le chatouillement est long-
temps continué, l'impression augmente de
manière qu'elle ébranle très-disagrèablement
les nerfs et la sensibilité.

3. La circulation et les mouvements
musculaires se font irrégulièrement—l'âme
même et la raison perdent leur empire.

4. Toute la machine est dans un état
violent, qui est accompagné de cris de

douleur, de spasmes, de convulsions, de
vomissements, de priapismes, d'évacuations
involuntaires de l'urine et de la semence ;
enfin, on a vu, plus d'une fois, cet état
contre nature, suivi de la mort.

SECTION III.

On the extremely horrible and agonising condition
to which a human being can be reduced by
systematic tickling.

· 1. THE following vivid description of the
exquisitely fiendish application of tickling
is an extract from the very interesting view
of modern society which is truly portrayed
in that remarkable production entitled
Valentine Vox, of which the principal and
most extraordinary incidents are founded on
facts concerning which the author (Mr.
Henry Cockton) made himself thoroughly
acquainted by personal investigation.

2. Mr. Goodman, the victim of the dia-

bolical treatment about to be described, had been placed in a private lunatic asylum by his own brother, on the altogether false pretence that he was insane and incapable of managing his affairs or taking care of himself; the real and only object being to possess his property.

3. Commissioners are legally appointed to visit these private asylums to ascertain the state of the inmates and to see that their treatment is both judicious and humane.

4. It was on the occasion of one of these visitations that the following scene occurred:—

5. Mr. Goodman, who is aware that the commissioners would shortly arrive, was preparing to prove to them that he was in the perfect possession of all his faculties, and felt confident that he would succeed and regain his liberty.

6. He had scarcely time to decide on the commencement of his address before the head keeper entered the yard where he was walking, and shouted to him—" Now then, here, you ! This way — here — you're wanted !"

*　　　*　　　*　　　*

7. Goodman joined him at once with the utmost firmness. He felt that all depended upon his tranquil bearing then, and hence determined not to notice any indignity that might be offered:

8. Instead, however, of being introduced to the commissioners, who were appropriately taking wine in the drawing-room, the keeper led him to the cell in which he slept, and in which he found another keeper loaded with an armful of chains.

"Now then !" shouted the principal ruffian, " come, strip ! and look alive !"

"Am I not to see the commissioners?" inquired Goodman calmly.

"And no mistake you are. They are coming directly. So you'd better look sharp."

"Pray," said Goodman, humbly yet earnestly, "allow me to see them as I am."

"Strip, I say, and be quick! D'ye hear me? Come, I'm not going to stand all this here dilly-dallying. Sam, here just lug off his coat." And the fellow threw the chains upon the ground and tore the coat off accordingly.

"My good man, pray tell me your in——"

"Silence!" interrupted the ruffian. "Hold your mouth, or I'll make yer!"

The very moment the coat was off they slipped on a strait-waistcoat, and then threw him down upon the bed; and while one of them was fastening an iron collar round his neck, and locking the chain attached to a stanchion, the other was engaged in pulling off his shoes and stockings, and chaining his legs firmly to the bottom of the bed.

Goodman remained silent. "Let them do what they please," thought he, "I shall still have the power to speak to the commissioners. Let them load me with chains. I must not be excited."

The sleeves of the strait-waistccat were now tied to the bedstead on either side; his bare feet were chained securely; he was unable to move hand or foot; he had not even the power to raise his head.

"Now," said the principal ruffian, addressing his assistant, "do you go down, and let me know when they're a-coming."

The fellow obeyed, and the moment he had done so the keeper deliberately drew a feather from his breast, and having straightened it, and looked at it with an air of the most intense satisfaction, knelt down at the foot of the bed.

"What, in Heaven's name," thought Goodman, "is about to take place? My good man," he exclaimed, in a state of alarm, "what—what are you going to do with me?"

Scarcely had the last word been uttered when the miscreant began to tickle the soles of his victim's feet.

"Oh! oh!" exclaimed Goodman. "Oh Do not! Pray do not! Oh, God! I cannot endure it! Mercy! Murder! Murder! Murder!" And he struggled and shrieked; and the more he shrieked and struggled the more quickly was the feather applied.

The blood rushed to his head. He strained horribly. The torture was exquisite. His cries might have pierced the heart even of a fiend; yet that wretch still kept on the dreadful process. "My God! my God!" exclaimed Goodman. "What agony!"

These were the last words he consciously uttered; for the veins began to swell, and his face became black, and his eyes appeared to be in the act of starting from their sockets. The room shook with his convulsions. He raved with maniacal fury. In a word, he had been goaded to madness.

"They are here!—they are here!" said the assistant, rushing into the room.

"All right—I've done the trick!" said the miscreant, concealing the feather, and throwing a blanket over the feet of his victim.

The commissioners entered. Goodman was a maniac, laughing and raving alternately—torturing his features into shapes the most hideous—writhing with frightful energy to get loose, and screaming horribly.

"Here is the poor man," observed the humane proprietor with an expression of the purest sympathy. "Poor gentleman! Really it is enough to make one's heart bleed to see him."

"Dreadful!" cried one of the commissioners.

"Dreadful indeed!" exclaimed another.

"Poor fellow! Is he often thus?" inquired a third.

"Not very often so out-and-out bad, sir," replied the brutal keeper; "only about twice a week, and he's much to be pitied. There aint a patient I pities more than him." And he winked at the proprietor, and the proprietor winked at him, as the commissioners drew near to the bedside, while poor Goodman was shouting, "Villains!—murder! —fiends!" He was mad—raving mad!

The commissioners were satisfied. Accustomed as they had been to such scenes, this struck them with horror, and they prepared to leave the room.

"It's shocking when they are so," observed the Christian proprietor, "truly shocking. Take care of him, Johnson; treat him tenderly, poor man!"

"I will, sir, depend on't," replied the keeper; and the commissioners quitted the room much affected.

The very moment they had left the miscreant burst into a loud roar of laughter, and congratulated himself on the success of his brutal experiment. He had tried it before frequently; and although one of his victims had died under the dreadful operation, while another had been struck with paralysis, and a third had been reduced to a state of idiotcy, in which he continued till death, it had occasionally so far failed as to induce almost immediate exhaustion, which had been found not to answer the proposed end so well.

In this case, however, he had been perfectly successful, and therefore, after having remained in the room until the commissioners had quitted the asylum, he left his raving victim with a fiend-like smile, to receive the applause of his infamous master.

SECTION IV.

On Mr. Darwin's opinions respecting laughter.

1. MR. DARWIN discusses the subject of laughter at considerable length in his extremely interesting volume on the *Expression of the Emotions.*

2. He there declares (p. 119) that idiots and imbecile persons afford good evidence that laughter or smiling primarily expresses mere happiness or joy.

3. He says—" Dr. Crichton Browne informs me that with idiots laughter is the most prevalent and frequent of all the emotional expressions.

4. " Many idiots are morose, passionate, restless, in a painful state of mind, or utterly

L

stolid, and these never laugh.   Others frequently laugh in a quite senseless manner.

5. " There is another large class of idiots who are persistently joyous and benign, and who are constantly laughing or smiling. Their countenances often exhibit a stereotyped smile.

6. " Their joyousness is increased, and they grin, chuckle, or giggle whenever food is placed before them, or when they are caressed, or are shown bright colours, or hear music.

7. " Some of them laugh more than usual when they walk about or attempt any muscular exertion.

8. " The joyousness of most of these idiots cannot possibly be associated (as Dr. Browne remarks) with any distinct ideas; they simply feel pleasure, and express it by laughter or smiles."

9. Our sincere conviction, after much experience and consideration, compels us to dissent from the opinion which is so distinctly expressed and reiterated in the above extract—namely, that laughter in idiots "primarily expresses mere happiness or joy;"—"they simply feel pleasure, and express it by laughter."

10. On the contrary, we are rather inclined to think that, on a careful and critical analysis of our various states of consciousness under any circumstances, it will be found that the experience of happiness, joy, or even pleasure (properly so called), never does manifest itself by bursts or fits of laughter.

In well-balanced and intelligent minds it certainly never does. We leave ill-regulated, ignorant, and vulgar minds altogether out of the question as not being fit subjects to reason upon or draw any inference from.

11. The fact appears simply to be this—
that in the case of every form of idiotcy the
brain and nervous system are irretrievably
diseased or deranged; the thoughts (if
thoughts they may be called) are altogether
irrational; the feelings are perverted and
unnatural.

12. Under these circumstances, and in
such a state of affliction, what kind or degree
of happiness, or joy, or pleasure can possibly
be realised?

13. They can unquestionably feel hunger
and thirst, and experience painful sensations,
but they can scarcely be said to think; and
what pleasure, may we ask, or what enter-
tainment can a human being enjoy who does
not possess the power of thought? He can
barely have a consciousness of his existence,
if even that.

14. In the foregoing extract from Mr.

Darwin laughing is shown to be a striking characteristic of idiotcy, and this exactly corroborates the theory set up in the preceding chapters of this treatise.

15. Sensible people—as may be observed every day—seldom laugh; and there are all degrees of laughers, from the wise and decorous, who rarely laugh, to the weak-minded fools, who very frequently laugh.

16. The laughing propensity gradually increases, in the same proportion as the weakness of mind increases, until we arrive at the lowest stage of mental vacuity, in which the habit of laughing becomes permanent and incessant.

17. It must be borne in mind that all the idiots and imbeciles who are referred to in Mr. Darwin's remarks were recklessly tomfooled in their infancy (in common with other children) by monkey tricks,

buffoonery, and tickling to make them laugh.

18. They thus got into the habit of laughing at an early age, and not possessing rational minds, they could not, of course, acquire any rational habits.

19. The silly, unmeaning habit of laughing, therefore, constitutes their only habit, and being so frequently exercised, becomes strengthened and inveterate, and, consequently, persistent and incessant.

LONDON:
PRINTED BY JAS. WADE, TAVISTOCK STREET, COVENT GARDEN.